Book 1
Quality Assurance
By Solis Tech

&

Book 2
Cryptography
By Solis Tech

&

Book 3
Human-Computer Interaction
By Solis Tech

Book 1
Quality Assurance

By Solis Tech

Software Quality Assurance Made Easy!

Quality Assurance: Software Quality Assurance Made Easy!

Table Of Contents

Introduction

I want to thank you and congratulate you for purchasing the book, *"Quality Assurance: Software Quality Assurance Made Easy"*.

This book contains proven steps and strategies on how to implement Software Quality Assurance.

Software quality assurance evolved from the quality assurance in industrial production in the 1940s. With the introduction of computers and the development of applications, it has become an important aspect of software development. In this book, you will learn about the various concepts of software quality assurance and its application in your workplace.

Chapter 1 talks about the definitions of software quality assurance and quality control. It is necessary that you understand what it is so that you can fully grasp the other fundamental concepts. Chapter 2 discusses the ways you can implement software quality assurance in an existing environment. In Chapter 3, you will learn how you can ensure that the software produces quality outputs.

Chapter 4 teaches you how to develop and run software testing while Chapter 5 talks about the timing of the software release. In Chapter 6, you will learn about using automated testing tools.

Thanks again for purchasing this book, I hope you enjoy it!

Chapter 1: Definition Of Software Quality Assurance And Software Testing

Software quality assurance is part of the process of software development. It includes the improvement and monitoring of the process. It also follows the processes, procedures, and standards. Furthermore, it ensures the resolution of problems discovered. In effect, it focuses on the prevention of problems.

Software testing, on the other hand, includes the operation of the application or system under controlled conditions, which must include all abnormal and normal conditions. The primary goal of software testing is to know what can go wrong when unexpected and expected scenarios occur. Its focus is on the detection of problems.

Companies differ in assigning responsibilities for quality assurance and software testing. There are organizations that combine both responsibilities to a single person or group. However, it is also common to have various teams that combine developers and testers. Project managers lead such teams. The decision to either combine or separate responsibilities depends on the company's business structure and size. Human beings or machines can perform software testing.

Some projects do not require a group of testers. The need for software testing depends on the project's context and size, the development methodology, the risks, the developers' experience and skill, and other factors. For example, a short-term, low-risk, and small project with expert developers, who know how to use test-first development or thorough unit testing, may not require software test engineers.

In addition, a small or new IT company may not have a dedicated software testing staff even its projects have a need for it. It may outsource software testing or use contractors. It may also adjust its approach on project development and management by using either agile test-first development or more experienced programmers. An inexperienced project manager may use his developers to do their own functional testing or skip thorough testing all together. This decision is highly risky and may cause the project to fail.

If the project is a huge one with non-trivial risks, software testing is important. The use of highly specialized software testers enhances the ability of the project to succeed because different people with different perspectives can offer their invaluable contribution because they have stronger and deeper skills.

In general, a software developer focuses on the technical issues to make a functionality work. On the other hand, a software test engineer focuses on what can go wrong with the functionality. It is very rare to come across a highly effective technical person, who can do both programming and testing tasks. As such, IT companies need software test engineers.

There are various reasons why software may have bugs. First, there is no communication or miscommunication as to the application's requirements. Second, the software is very complex so an inexperienced individual may have a difficult time understanding the software application. In addition, the software may be a big one and includes big databases, data communications, security complexities, different remote and local web services, and multi-tier distributed systems.

Third, there are programming errors. Fourth, the requirements of the software change because the end-user requests for them. In some cases, this end-user may not be aware of the effects of such changes, which can result in errors. The staff's enthusiasm is affected. Continuous modification requirements are a reality. Quality assurance and software test engineers must be able to plan and adapt continuous testing to prevent bugs from affecting the software.

Fifth, time pressures can be difficult to manage. Mistakes often occur during crunch times. Sixth, people involved in the project may not be able to manage their own egos. Seventh, the code has poor documentation or design. It is difficult to modify and maintain codes that are poorly written or documented. Bugs can occur if IT companies do not offer incentives for developers to write maintainable, understandable, and clear codes. Most companies offer incentives when they are able to finish the code quickly. Eighth, the use of software development tools can also result to bugs.

How Quality Assurance Evolved

In 1946, the US Occupation Forces established the Quality Movement in Japan. The movement follows the research of W. Edwards Deming and the Statistical Process Control papers. The methods discussed by the research and papers pertained to industrial production. Each process of production has an output with a required specification and a verifiable main product. The Quality Control group measures the output at different production stages. It ensures that the output falls within the acceptable variances.

The Quality Assurance group does not part in the production process. It audits the process to ensure compliance with the established standards and guidelines. It gives its input for the continuous improvement of the process. In a manufacturing setup, it is easy to differentiate between quality assurance and quality control. These methods become the norm in manufacturing. Since they work in industrial production, they spawned the birth of software quality control and software quality assurance.

Quality Attributes Of Software

Hewlett Packard's Robert Grady developed the common definition of the Software Quality Attributes. The FURPS model identified the following characteristics: functionality, usability, reliability, performance, and supportability (FURPS).

The functional attributes pertain to the features of the software. They answer the question about the purpose of the software instead of its use. The reason for the software's existence is different from the concerns about its reliability, look and feel, and security. The usability attributes are characteristics pertaining to user interface issues like consistency, interface aesthetics, and accessibility.

The reliability attributes include recoverability, accuracy, and availability of the system while performance attributes pertain to issues like startup time, recovery time, system response time, and information throughput. Supportability addresses issues like localizability, scalability, installation, configurability, compatibility, maintainability, adaptability, and testability. The FURPS model evolved into FURPS+ to include specification of constraints like physical, interface, implementation, and design constraints.

The Software Quality Control team tests the quality characteristics. The tests for usability and functionality occur during execution of the actual software. On the other hand, adaptability and supportability tests occur through code inspection. It is not the responsibility of the Software Quality Control or Software Quality Assurance to put the quality attributes into the software. The Software Quality Control team tests for the absence or presence of such characteristics while the Software Quality Assurance group ensures that each stakeholder follow the right standards and procedures during software execution.

In theory, the implementation of FURPS+ will overcome the problems caused by the software's intangible nature because the Software Quality Control team can measure each software attribute. For example, the amount of time it takes for programmers to fix a bug is a measure of supportability. To improve it requires the implementation of new coding standards.

The Software Quality Control group can inspect the code to ensure compliance with the coding standard while the Software Quality Assurance team can ensure that the quality control and programmer teams follow the right standards and process. It is the duty of the Software Quality Assurance group to collect and analyze the time spent on fixing the bug so that it can provide an input in terms of its usefulness to the process improvement initiative.

Chapter 2: Introducing Software Quality Assurance Procedures To An Existing Company

The introduction of the software quality assurance procedures rely on the risks involved and the company's size. If the organization is large and the projects are high-risk, the management must consider a more formal quality assurance process. On the other hand, if the risk is lower, the implementation of quality assurance may be a step-at-a-time procedure. The processes of quality assurance maintain balance with productivity.

If the project or the company is small, an ad-hoc process may be more appropriate. The success of the software development relies on the team leaders and developers. More importantly, there must be enough communications between software testers, managers, customers, and developers. Requirement specifications must be complete, testable, and clear. There must be procedures for design and code reviews, as well as retrospectives. Common approaches used are Agile, Kaizen, and Deming-Shewhart Plan-Do-Check-Act methods.

It is important to evaluate documents, code, specifications, plans, and requirements. To do this, it is necessary to prepare issues lists, checklists, inspection meetings, and walkthroughs. This process is what IT people refer to as verification. On the other hand, validation occurs after verification and includes actual testing of the application. A walkthrough is evaluation in an informal meeting. There is no need to prepare for it.

An inspection is more formal than a walkthrough and attended by at most eight people including a reader, a recorder, and a moderator. Usually, an inspection's subject is a test plan or requirements specification so that the attendees will know the software's problems. The attendees must read the document before attending an inspection so they will find the problems prior to the meeting. It is difficult to prepare for an inspection but it is an effective and least costly way to ensure quality.

Testing Requirements That Must Be Considered

The basis of black box testing is the software's functionality and requirements. A software tester need not be knowledgeable of code or internal design. White box testing, on the other hand, requires knowledge of code. It takes into consideration the code statements, paths, branches, and conditions. Unit testing requires testing of particular code modules or functions. Usually, the application developer performs it because it requires detailed knowledge of the code and program design.

API testing is testing of data exchange or messaging among systems parts. An incremental integration testing tests the application when there is a new functionality, which must be independent to work separately before it can be included in the application. The application programmer or software tester performs this type of testing. An integration testing requires the testing of the various parts of the software in order to know if they work together properly. Functional testing, on the other hand, is a kind of black box testing that focuses on the application's functional requirements. The software testers perform it.

System testing is also another type of black box testing. It includes testing of the general requirements specifications and all the various parts of the software. End-to-end testing, on the other hand, is a macro type of system testing. It includes testing the whole software in various situations that replicates real-world use. Smoke testing or sanity testing is an initial testing to know if the new version is performing well so that major testing can commence. Regression testing retests the application after some modifications or fixes.

Acceptance testing is final testing the software based on customer's specifications. Load testing is software testing under heavy loads in order to find out when the response time of the system fails or degrades. Stress testing, on the other hand, is system functional testing with unusually heavy loads, large complex queries of the database, using large numerical values, and heavy repetition of certain inputs or actions. Performance testing is testing using test or quality assurance plans.

The goal of usability testing depends on the customer or end-user. It uses techniques like surveys, user interviews, and user sessions' video recording. Software testers and developers are not the people to implement usability testing. Install/uninstall testing uses processes to test upgrade, full, or partial install/uninstall of the software. Recovery testing determines how the software can recover in catastrophic instances like hardware failures and crashes. Failover testing is another name for recovery testing.

Security testing tests how the application protects against willful damage, unauthorized access, and the likes. It uses sophisticated testing methods. Compatibility testing tests how the application performs in some environments. Exploratory testing, on the other hand, is an informal and creative testing that does not use any formal test cases or plans. Usually, software testers are new to the application. Ad-hoc testing is almost the same as exploratory testing but the software testers understand the application prior to testing.

Context-driven testing focuses on the software's intended use, culture, and environment. For example, medical equipment software has a different testing approach than a computer game. User acceptance testing determines if the application is satisfactory to the customer or end-user. Comparison testing, on the other hand, compares the software with its competitors.

Alpha testing occurs when the software is almost finished. Usually, end users perform this type of testing. Beta testing is testing when the software is finished and ready for final release. Like alpha testing, this kind of testing is for end users. Finally, mutation testing uses test cases and allows for code changes and retesting using the original test cases to discover software bugs.

Common Problems And Solutions In Developing Software

Software development can encounter common problems like poor user stories or requirements, unrealistic schedule, inadequate testing, featuritis, and miscommunication. Problems can arise if there requirements are incomplete, unclear, not testable, or too general. Furthermore, if the software development has a short timetable, problems can also be evident. If the software does not pass through the testing process, the IT organization will only know of problems if the system crashes or the end users complain.

In addition, problems can arise if the users or customers request for more new functionalities even after the development goals are set. Finally, if there is miscommunication between the programmers and customers, problems are inevitable. If it is an agile project, the problems become evident when it strays away from agile principles.

If there are common problem then there are also common solutions like solid requirements, realistic schedules, adequate testing, sticking to original requirements, and communication. Software requirements must be complete, clear, cohesive, detailed, testable, and attainable. All players concerned must agree upon them. In agile environments, there must be close coordination with end users or customers so that any change in requirement is clear. There must be enough time for design, planning, bug fixing, testing, changes, retesting, and documentation. Each person must not feel burnout during the project.

For testing to be adequate, it must start early. Retesting must occur after each change or fix. There must be enough time for bug fixing and testing. If the end user or customer requests for excessive changes when development has begun, it is important that the project manager explain the consequences. If the change is important, a schedule change is inevitable to accommodate it.

The project manager must manage the expectations of the end users or customer. In an agile environment, the project manager can expect significant change in the initial requirements. There must be a schedule for inspections and walkthroughs. The use of communication tools is important to ensure cooperation and teamwork.

Software Quality Assurance And Software Quality Control In The Workplace

If there is no formal implementation of Software Quality Assurance/Software Quality Control, the quality group can mirror that of an engineering services group. It performs the tasks not done by the development team. It reports to the application development manager. Under this scenario, the manager can instruct the quality assurance personnel to install a load-testing tool and declare him as a performance expert. Although the quality assurance person must perform load testing, it is the job of the software designer/programmer. As such, the software quality assurance/software quality control must be separate from the development team.

Software quality assurance requires the establishment of templates used during reviews. Such templates must have sections for both non-functional and functional requirements. For example, the requirements for performance must be in terms of transaction rates and user population. The use of Traceability Matrix can help in the requirements management. The matrix also encourages the analyst to use individual requirements for cross-referencing.

Software quality assurance verifies that the requirements comply with the templates and that they are not ambiguous. It reviews the risks of non-completion of the non-functional attributes, as well as the Traceability Matrix, to ensure usability of all requirements in other specifications. Software quality assurance can write the test cases, which refer to some of the requirements. It can cross-reference the requirements in the Traceability Matrix.

The interface specification is a requirement if the software is component-based. Software quality assurance must subject the document to verification. It must also subject other lower level specifications to quality assurance if such requirements are critical. Even if there are limited resources for software quality assurance, an IT organization can obtain a good return-on-investment if it pays attention to requirements and interfaces.

Chapter 3: Ensuring Software Quality

Software quality is the delivery of bug-free software within budget and on time. Because quality is subjective, it depends on the customer and his overall influence in the project. A customer can be an end user, a customer contract officer, a customer acceptance tester, a customer manager, a software maintenance engineer, and others. Each customer has his own definition of quality.

A code is good if it works, is secure, bug free, maintainable, and readable. Some companies have standards, which their programmers follow. However, each developer has his own idea about what is best. Standards have different metrics and theories. If there are excessive rules and standards, they can limit creativity and productivity. A design can be functional or internal design.

An internal design is good if the overall structure of the software code is clear, easily modifiable, understandable, and maintainable. It is robust with the capability to log status and with sufficient error handling. Furthermore, the software works as expected. A functional design is good if the software functionality comes from the requirements of the end user and customer. Even an inexperienced user can use the software without reading the user manual or seeking online help.

The software life cycle starts with the conception of the application and commences when the software is no longer used. It includes factors like requirements analysis, initial concept, internal design, functional design, test planning, documentation planning, document preparation, coding, maintenance, testing, integration, retesting, updates, and phase out.

A good software test engineer must possess a test to break attitude, which means that he must be able to focus on the detail in order to ensure that the application is of good quality. He must be diplomatic and tactful so that he can maintain a good relationship with the programmers, the customers, and the managements.

It is helpful if he has previous experience on software development so that he understands the whole process deeply. A good software test engineer is able to appreciate the point of view of the programmers. He must have good judgment skills to be able to determine critical or high-risk application areas that require testing.

A good quality assurance engineer also shares the same qualities with a good software test engineer. Furthermore, he must understand the whole process of software development and the organizations' goals and business approach. He must possess understanding of all sides of issues in order to communicate effectively with everyone concerned. He must be diplomatic and patient, especially in the early stages of the quality assurance process. Lastly, he must be able to detect problems during inspections and reviews.

Qualities Of A Good Quality Assurance Or Test Manager

A good manager must be familiar with the process of software development and must be enthusiastic and promote positivity in the team. He must be able to increase productivity by promoting teamwork and cooperation between quality assurance, software, and test engineers. If the processes require improvements, he must be diplomatic in ensuring smooth implementation of such changes.

He must be able to withstand pressure and offer the right feedback about quality issues to the other managers. He must be able to hire and keep the right personnel. He must possess strong communication skills to deal with everyone concerned in the process. Lastly, he must stay focused and be able to hold meetings.

Importance Of Documentation In Quality Assurance

If the team is large, it is more useful to have the proper documentation for efficient communication and management of projects. Documentation of quality assurance practices is necessary for repeatability. Designs, specifications, configurations, business rules, test plans, code changes, bug reports, test cases, and user manuals must have proper documentation. A system of documentation is necessary for easy obtaining and finding of information.

Each project has its own requirements. If it is an agile project, the requirements may change and evolve. Thus, there is no need for detailed documentation. However, it is useful to document user stories. Documentation on the software requirements describes the functionality and properties of the software. It must be clear, reasonably detailed, complete, attainable, cohesive, and testable. It may be difficult to organize and determine the details but there are tools and methods that are available.

It is important to exercise care in documenting the requirements of the project's customer, who may be an outside or in-house personnel, an end user, a customer contract officer, a customer acceptance tester, a customer manager, a sales person, or a software maintenance engineer. If the project did not meet the expectations, any of these customers can slow down the project.

Each organization has its own way of handling requirements. If the project is an agile project, the requirements are in the user stories. On the other hand, for other projects, the requirements are in the document. Some organizations may use functional specification and high-level project plans. In every requirement, documentation is important to help software testers to make test plans and perform testing. Without any significant documentation, it is impossible to determine if the application meets the user expectations.

Even if the requirements are not testable, it is still important to test the software. The test results must be oriented towards providing information about the risk levels and the status of the application. It is significant to have the correct testing approach to ensure success of the project. In an agile project, various approaches can use methods that require close cooperation and interaction among stakeholders.

Chapter 4: How To Develop And Run Software Testing

To develop the steps for software testing, it is necessary to consider the following.

First, it is important to get the requirements, user stories, internal design, functional design, and any other information that can help with the testing process.

Second, testing must have budget and schedule.

Third, it must have personnel with clear responsibilities.

Fourth, there must be project context to determine testing approaches, scope, and methods.

Fifth, identification of limitations and scope of tests is necessary in order to set priorities.

Sixth, testing must include methods and approaches applicable.

Seventh, it must have the requirements to determine the test environment.

Eighth, it must have requirements for testing tools.

Ninth, it is important to determine the data requirements for testing input.

Tenth, identification of labor requirements and tasks are important.

Eleventh, it must determine milestones, timelines, and schedule estimates.

Twelfth, testing must include error classes, boundary value analysis, and input equivalence classes, when needed.

Thirteenth, it must have a test plan and documents for approvals and reviews.

Fourteenth, testing must determine test scenarios and cases.

Fifteenth, it must include reviews, approvals of test cases, inspections, approaches, and scenarios.

Sixteenth, there must be testing tools and test environment, user manuals, configuration guides, reference documents, installation guides, test tracking processes, archiving and logging processes, and test input data.

Seventeenth, it must include software releases,

The Test Plan

A test plan is a document, which includes scope, objectives, and focus of the software testing activity. To prepare it, it is important to consider the efforts needed to validate the software's acceptability. The test plan must help even those people who are not part of the test group. Testing must be thorough but not very detailed.

The test plan can include the following: the title, the software version number, the plan's revision history, table of contents, the intended audience, the goal of testing, the overview of the software, relevant documents, legal or standards requirements, identifier and naming standards, and requirements for traceability. The test plan must also include overall project organization, test organization, dependencies and assumptions, risk analysis of the project, focus and priorities of testing, limitations and scope, test outline, data input outline, test environment, analysis of test environment validity, configuration and setup of test environment, and processes for software migration among other things.

A test case includes the input, event, or action plus its expected result in order to know if software's functionality is working as planned. It contains test case identifier, objective, test case name, test setup, requirements for input data, steps, and expected results. The details may differ, depending on the project context and organization. Some organizations handle test cases differently. Most of them use less-detailed test scenarios for simplicity and adaptability of test documentation. It is important to develop test cases because it is possible to detect problems and errors in the software through them.

When A Bug Is Discovered

If the software has a bug, the programmers must fix it. The software must undergo retesting after the resolution of the error. Regression testing must be able to check that the solutions performed were not able to create more problems within the application. A system for problem tracking must be set up so it becomes easier to perform the retesting. There are various software tools available to help the quality assurance team.

In tracking the problems, it is good to consider the following: complete information about the bug, bug identifier, present bug status, software version number, how the bug was discovered, specifics about environment and hardware, test case information, bug description, cause of the bug, fix description, retesting results, etc. There must be a reporting process so that the appropriate personnel will know about the errors and fixes.

A configuration management includes the various processes used to coordinate, control, and track requirements, code, problems, documentation, designs, change requests, tools, changes made, and person who made the changes. If the software has many bugs, the software tester must report them and focus on critical bugs. Because this problem can affect the schedule, the software tester must inform the managers and send documentation in order to substantiate the problem.

The decision to stop testing is difficult to do, especially for complex applications. In some cases, complete testing is not possible. Usually, the decision to stop testing considers the deadlines, the degree of test cases completion, the depletion of the test budget, the specified coverage of code, the reduction of the bug rate, and the ending of alpha or beta testing periods. If there is not enough time to perform thorough testing, it is important to focus the testing on important matters based on risk analysis. If the project is small, the testing can depend on risk analysis again.

In some cases, there are organizations that are not serious about quality assurance. For them, it is important to solve problems rather than prevent problems. Problems regarding software quality may not be evident. Furthermore, some organizations reward people who fix problems instead of incentivizing prevention of problems. Risk management includes actions that prevent things from happening. It is a shared responsibility among stakeholders. However, there must be a point person who is primarily responsible for it. In most cases, the responsibility falls on the quality assurance personnel.

Chapter 5: Deciding When To Release The Software To Users

In most projects, the decision to release the software depends on the timing of the end testing. However, for most applications, it is difficult to specify the release criteria without using subjectivity and assumptions. If the basis of the release criteria is the result of a specific test, there is an assumption that this test has addressed all the necessary software risks.

For many projects, this is impossible to do without incurring huge expenses. Therefore, the decision is actually a leap of faith. Furthermore, most projects try to balance cost, timeliness, and quality. As such, testing cannot address the balance of such factors when there is a need to decide on the release date.

Usually, the quality assurance or test manager decides when to release the software. However, this decision involves various assumptions. First, the test manager understands the considerations, which are significant in determining the quality of the software to justify release. Second, the quality of the software may not balance with cost and timeliness. In most organization, there is not enough definition for sufficient quality. Thus, it becomes very subjective and may vary from day to day or project to project.

The release criteria must consider the sales goals, deadlines, market considerations, legal requirements, quality norms of the business segment, programming and technical considerations, expectations of end users, internal budget, impact on the other projects, and a host of other factors. Usually, the project manager must know all these factors.

Because of the various considerations, it may not be possible for the quality assurance manager or test manager to decide the release of the software. However, he may be responsible in providing inputs to the project manager, who makes the release decision. If the project or the organization is small, the decision to release the software rests on the project manager or the product manager. For larger organizations or projects, there must be a committee to decide when to release the software.

If the software requirements change continuously, it is important for all stakeholders to cooperate from the beginning so that they all understand how the change in requirements may affect the project. They may decide on alternate strategies and test plans in advance. It is also beneficial to the project if the initial design of the software can accommodate changes later on. A well-documented code makes it easier for programmers to make the necessary changes.

It is also good to use rapid prototyping if possible so that customers will not make more requests for changes because they are sure of their requirements from the very beginning. The initial schedule of the project must allow extra lead-time for these changes. If possible, all changes must be in the "Phase 2" of the software version. It is important that only easily implemented requirements must be in the project.

The difficult ones must be in the future versions. The management and the customers must know about costs, inherent risks, and scheduling impacts of big changes in the requirements. If they know about the challenges, they can decide whether to continue with the changes or not.

There must be balance between expected efforts with the effort to set up automated testing for the changes. The design of the automated test scripts must be flexible. Its focus must be on aspects of application, which will remain unchanged. The reduction of the appropriate effort for the risk analysis of the changes can be through regression testing.

The design of the test cases must be flexible. The focus must be on ad-hoc testing and not on detailed test cases and test plans. If there is a continuous request for changes in the requirements, it is unreasonable to expect that requirements will remain stable and pre-determined. Thus, it may be appropriate to use approaches for agile development.

It is difficult to determine if software has significant hidden or unexpected functionality. It also indicates that the software development process has deeper problems. The functionality must be removed if does not serve any purpose to the software because it may have unknown dependencies or impacts. If not removed, there must be a consideration for the determination of regression testing needs and risks. The management must know if there are significant risks caused by the unexpected functionality.

The implementation of quality assurance processes is slow over time because the stakeholders must have a consensus. There must be an alignment of processes and organizational goals. As the organization matures, there will be an improvement on productivity. Problem prevention will be the focus. There will be a reduction of burnout and panics. There will be less wasted effort and more improved focus.

The processes must be efficient and simple to prevent any "Process Police" mentality. Furthermore, quality assurance processes promote automated reporting and tracking thereby minimizing paperwork. However, in the short run, implementation may be slow. There will be more days for inspections, reviews, and planning but less time for handling angry end users and late night fixing of errors.

If the growth of the IT organization is very rapid, fixed quality assurance processes may be impossible. Thus, it is important to hire experienced people. The management must prioritize issues about quality and maintain a good relationship with the customers. Every employee must know what quality means to the end user.

Chapter 6: Using Automated Testing Tools

If the project is small, learning and implementing the automated testing tools may not be worth it. However, these automated testing tools are important for large projects. These tools use a standard coding language like Java, ruby, python, or other proprietary scripting language. In some cases, it is necessary to record the first tests for the generation of the test scripts. Automated testing is challenging if there are continuous changes to the software because a change in test code is necessary every time there is a new requirement. In addition, the analysis and interpretation of results can be difficult.

Data driven or keyword driven testing is common in functional testing. The maintenance of actions and data is easy through a spreadsheet. The test drivers read the information for them to perform the required tests. This strategy provides more control, documentation, development, and maintenance of test cases. Automated tools can include code analyzers, coverage analyzers, memory analyzers, load/performance test tools, web test tools, and other tools.

A test engineer, who does manual testing, determines if the application performs as expected. He must be able to judge the expected outcome. However, in an automated test, the computer judges the test outcome. A mechanism must be present for the computer to compare automatically between the actual and expected outcomes for every test scenario. If the test engineer is new to automated testing, it is important that he undergo training first.

Proper planning and analysis are important in selecting and using an automated tool for testing. The right tool must be able to test more thoroughly than manual methods. It must test faster and allow continuous integration. It must also reduce the tedious manual testing. The automation of testing is costly. However, it may be able to provide savings in the long term.

Choosing The Appropriate Test Environment

There is always a tradeoff between cost and test environment. The ultimate scenario is to have a collection of test environments, which mirror exactly all possible usage, data, network, software, and hardware characteristics that the software can use. For most software, it is impossible to predict all environment variations. Furthermore, for complex and large systems, it is extremely expensive to duplicate a live environment.

The reality is that decisions on the software environment characteristics are important. Furthermore, the choice of test environments takes into consideration logistical, budget, and time constraints. People with the most technical experience and knowledge, as well as with the deep understanding of constraints and risks, make these decisions. If the project is low risk or small, it is common to take the informal approach. However, for high risk or large projects, it is important to take a more formalize procedure with many personnel.

It is also possible to coordinate internal testing with efforts for beta testing. In addition, it is possible to create built-in automated tests upon software installation by users. The tests are able to report information through the internet about problems and application environment encountered. Lastly, it is possible to use virtual environments.

The Best Approach To Test Estimation

It is not easy to find the best approach because it depends on the IT organization, the project, as well as the experience of the people involved. If there are two projects with the same size and complexity, the right test effort for life-critical medical software may be very large compared to a project involving an inexpensive computer game. The choice of a test estimation approach based on complexity and size may be applicable to a project but not to the other one.

The implicit risk context approach caters to a quality assurance manager or project manager, who uses risk context with past personal experiences to allocate resources for testing. The risk context assumes that each project is similar to the others. It is an experience-based intuitive guess.

The metrics-based approach, on the other hand, uses past experiences on different projects. If there is already data from a number of projects, the information is beneficial in future test planning. For each new project, the basis of adjustment of required test time is the available metrics. In essence, this is not easy to do because it is judgment based on historical experience.

The test-work breakdown approach decomposes the testing tasks into smaller tasks to estimate testing with a reasonable accuracy. It assumes that the breakdown of testing tasks is predictable and accurate and that it is feasible to estimate the testing effort. If the project is large, this is not feasible because there is a need to extend testing time if there are many bugs. In addition to, there is a need to extend development time.

The iterative approach is for large test projects. An initial rough estimate is necessary prior to testing. Once testing begins and after finishing a small percentage of testing work, there is a need to update the testing estimate because testers have already obtained additional knowledge of the issues, risks, and software quality. There is also a need to update test schedules and plans. After finishing a larger percentage of testing work, the testing estimate requires another update. The cycle continues until testing ends.

The percentage-of-development approach requires a quick way of testing estimation. If the project has 1,000 hours of estimated programming effort, the

IT firm usually assigns a 40% ratio for testing. Therefore, it will allot 400 hours for testing. The usefulness of this approach depends on risk, software type, personnel, and complexity level.

In an agile software development approach, the test estimate is unnecessary if the project uses pure test-driven development although it is common to mix some automated unit tests with either automated or manual functional testing. By the nature of agile-based projects, they are not dependent on testing efforts but on the construction of the software.

Conclusion

Thank you again for purchasing this book!

I hope this book was able to help you to understand the concepts of Software Quality Assurance.

The next step is to apply what you learned from this book to your work.

Finally, if you enjoyed this book, please take the time to share your thoughts and post a review on Amazon. It'd be greatly appreciated!

Thank you and good luck!

Book 2
Cryptography
By Solis Tech

Cryptography Theory & Practice Made Easy!

Cryptography: Cryptography Theory & Practice Made Easy!

Table of Contents

Introduction

I want to thank you and congratulate you for purchasing the book, *Cryptography*.

This book contains tips and techniques on how to build cryptosystems – even if you're just a complete beginner.

This eBook will help you learn about the history and basic principles of cryptography. It will teach you the different aspects of message encryption. In addition, you will learn how to establish cryptosystems. Aside from discussing modern/digital encryption schemes, this book will teach you how to use different types of "practical" ciphers.

Thanks again for purchasing this book. I hope you enjoy it!

Chapter 1: Cryptography – History and Basic Concepts

The Origin of Cryptography

During the ancient times, people needed to do two things: (1) to share information and (2) protect the information they are sharing. These things forced individuals to "encode" their messages. This "encoding" process protects the message in a way that only the intended recipient can understand the information. That means the data will remain secure even if unauthorized parties get access to it.

The art and science of protecting information is now known as "cryptography." The term "cryptography" was formed by fusing two Greek terms, "Krypto" (which means "hidden") and "graphene" (which means writing).

According to historians, cryptography and "normal" writing were born at the same time. As human civilizations progressed, people organized themselves into groups, clans, and kingdoms. These organizations led to the creation of concepts such as wars, powers, sovereignty, and politics. Obviously, these ideas involve information that cannot be shared with ordinary citizens. The group leaders needed to send and receive information through protected means. Thus, cryptography continued to evolve.

The Contributions of Egyptians and Romans

1. Egyptians

The oldest sample of cryptography can be found in Egypt. Ancient Egyptians used hieroglyphs (i.e. a system of writing that involves symbols and images) to share and record pieces of information. In general, these symbols and images are only intelligible to the priests who transmitted messages on behalf of the pharaohs. Here is a sample hieroglyph:

Fig. 1 - Egyptian Hieroglyphs

Several thousands of years later (around 600 to 500 BC), Egyptian scholars started to use simple substitution codes. This style of encoding involved the replacement and/or combination of two or more alphabets using a secret rule. This rule was considered as the "key" in retrieving the real message from the coded "garbage."

2. Romans

Ancient Romans used a system of cryptography known as the Caesar (or Shift) Cipher. This system depends on moving each letter of the message by a certain number (three is the most popular choice). To decode the information, the recipient simply needs to "move" the letters back using the same number. Here is an example:

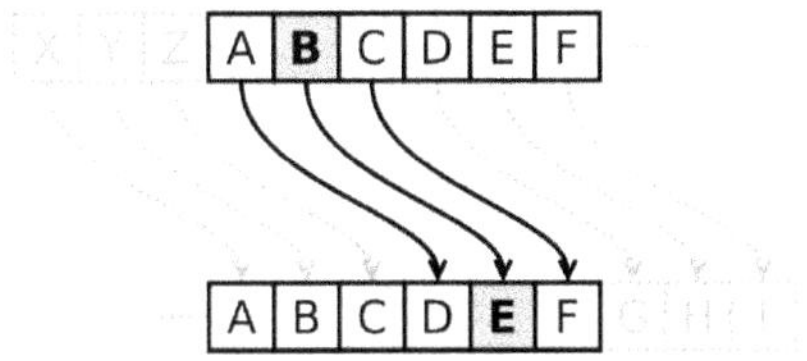

Fig. 2 – Caesar Cipher

Cryptography - Fundamental Concepts

Encryption – This is the process of converting information into an unintelligible form. It helps in securing the privacy of the message while it is being sent to the recipient.

Decryption – This process is the exact opposite of encryption. Here, the encoded message is returned to its natural form.

Important Note: Encryption and decryption requires specific rules in converting the data involved. These rules are known as the key. Sometimes, a single key is used to encrypt and decrypt information. However, there are certain scenarios where these two processes require different sets of keys.

Plaintext and Ciphertext – The term plaintext refers to data that can be read and used without the application of special techniques. Ciphertext, on the other hand, refers to data that cannot be read easily: the recipient needs to use certain decryption processes to get the "real" message.

Authentication – This is probably one of the most important aspects of cryptography. Basically, authentication serves as a proof that the information was sent by the party claimed in the encoded message.]

Let's illustrate this concept using a simple example: John sent a message to Jane. However, before replying, Jane wants to make sure that the message really came from John. This verification procedure can be conducted easily if John does "something" on the message that Jane knows only John can do (e.g. writing his signature, including a secret phrase, folding the letter in a certain way, etc.). Obviously, successful decryption of the message will be useless if the information came from an unwanted source.

Integrity – Loss of integrity is one of the biggest problems faced by people who use cryptography. Basically, loss of integrity occurs whenever the message gets altered while it is being sent to the receiver. Unnecessary and/or unwanted modifications in a message may cause misunderstanding and other issues. Because of this, the message must be protected while it is being delivered. Modern cryptographers accomplish this through the use of a cryptographic hash (i.e. a hash function that is extremely difficult to invert, modify, or recreate).

Non-Repudiation – This concept focuses on ensuring that the sender cannot deny that he/she sent the encoded message. In the example given above, it is important to make sure that John cannot deny the fact that he was the one who sent the message. Modern cryptography prevents this "sender repudiation" using digital signatures.

Chapter 2: The Modern Cryptography

For some people, modern cryptography is the foundation of technology and communications security. This type of cryptography is based on mathematical concepts like the number theory, the probability theory, and the computational-complexity theory. To help you understand modern cryptography, here is a comparison of the "classical" and "modern" types of cryptography.

Classical Cryptography

1. It utilizes common characters (e.g. letters and numbers) directly.

2. It relies heavily on the "obscure is secure" principle. The encryption and decryption processes were considered as confidential information. Only the people involved in the communication can access such data.

3. It needs an entire cryptosystem (will be explained in the next chapter) to complete the "confidential" transfer of information.

Modern Cryptography

1. It relies on modern technology like binary data sequences.

2. The information is encoded through the use of mathematical algorithms accessible to the public. Here, security is achieved through a "secret key" which is used as the foundation for the algorithms. Two factors ensure that "outsiders" cannot access the information even if they have the correct algorithm:

    a. It is extremely difficult to compute such algorithms. Thus, it is hard to extract any information from them.

    b. The absence or presence of secret keys.

3. The encryption doesn't involve the entire cryptosystem. Only the interested parties are required to participate in encoding and decoding the message.

Chapter 3: Cryptosystem - The Basics

A cryptosystem is the application of cryptographic methods and their appropriate coding environment (also called "infrastructure"). This system is used to add security to technology and communications services. Some people refer to cryptosystems as "cipher systems."

To illustrate the concept of cryptosystems, let's consider the following example:

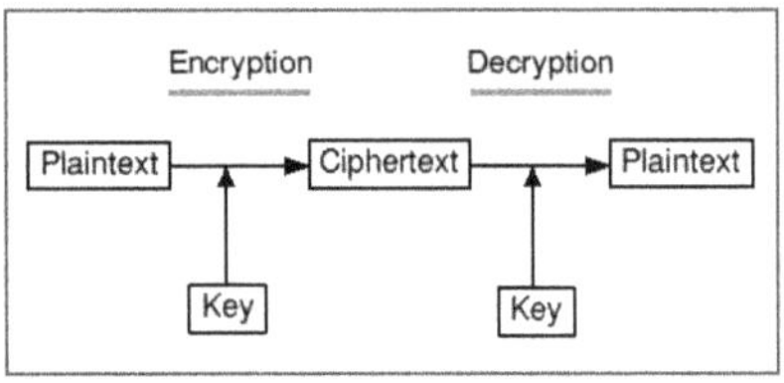

Fig. 3 – A Cryptosystem

In this example, the sender encrypts his message (i.e. the plaintext) through the use of a key. This process converts the plaintext into ciphertext. Once the receiver gets the ciphertext, he uses the same key to decrypt the information. Thus, the ciphertext will be turned into plaintext again.

As you can see, only the parties who have the "key" can access the shared information. Cryptosystems can be divided into these basic components:

- Plaintext – The information that needs to be shared and protected.
- Encryption Algorithm – The mathematical process that uses a plaintext and an encryption key to produce a ciphertext.
- Ciphertext – The coded version of the information. In general, cryptography protects the message itself, not the transmission. That means the coded message is sent through public channels such as emails. Thus, anyone who can access the selected delivery channel can intercept or compromise the message.
- Decryption Algorithm – It is a mathematical process that creates plaintext from any given set of ciphertext and decryption key. Basically, it reverses the encryption process done earlier in the transmission of the message.

- Encryption Key – The value provided by the sender. In creating the ciphertext, the sender enters this key (along with the plaintext) into the encryption algorithm.
- Decryption Key – The value known by the recipient. The decryption key is always related to the encryption key used for the message. However, these keys don't have to be identical. The recipient enters the decryption key and the ciphertext into the decryption algorithm in order to get the plaintext. The collection of all decryption keys for a cryptosystem is known as a "key space."

There are times when an interceptor (also called "attacker") tries to get the encoded message. In general, interceptors are unauthorized entities who want to access the ciphertext and determine the information it contains.

The Two Kinds of Cryptosystems

Currently, cryptosystems are divided into two kinds: (1) Symmetric Key Encryption and (2) Asymmetric Key Encryption. This way of classifying cryptosystems is based on the method of encryption/decryption used for the entire system.

The major difference between the symmetric and asymmetric encryptions is the connection between the encryption and decryption keys. Generally speaking, all cryptosystems involve keys that are closely related. It is impossible to create a decryption key that is totally unrelated to the code's encryption key. Let's discuss each kind of cryptosystems in more detail:

Symmetric Key Encryption

Cryptosystems that belong to this kind have a single key. This key is used to encrypt and decrypt the information being sent. The study of symmetric encryption and systems is known as "symmetric cryptography." Some people refer to symmetric cryptosystems as "secret key" systems. The most popular methods of symmetric key encryption are: IDEA, BLOWFISH, DES (Digital Encryption Standard), and 3DES (Triple-DES).

During the 1960s, 100% of the cryptosystems utilized symmetric encryption. This method of encrypting and decrypting information is so reliable and efficient that it is still being used even today. Businesses that specialize on Communications and Information Technology consider symmetric encryption as the best option available. Since this kind of encryption has distinct advantages over the asymmetric one, it will still be used in the future.

Here are the main characteristics of symmetrically encrypted cryptosystems:

- Before transmitting the message, the sender and the receiver must determine the key that will be used.
- The key must be changed regularly to avoid any intrusion into the cryptosystem.
- A stable form of data transmission must be established to facilitate easy sharing of the key between the involved parties. Since the keys must be changed on a regular basis, this mechanism may prove to be expensive and complicated.
- In an organization composed of "x" individuals, to facilitate two-way communication between any two members, the required number of keys for the entire system is derived using the formula: "x * (x-1)/2."
- The keys used are often small (i.e. measured through the number of bits involved), so the encryption and decryption processes are faster and simpler compared to those used for asymmetric systems.
- These cryptosystems do not require high processing capabilities from computer systems. Since the keys used are small and simple, ordinary computers can be used to establish and manage the cryptosystem.

Here are the two problems usually encountered when using this kind of cryptosystem:

- Key Determination – Before any message can be transmitted, the sender and the receiver must determine a specific symmetric key. That means a secure and consistent way of creating keys must be established.
- Trust Issues – Because all the people involved use the same key, symmetric key cryptography requires the sender to trust the receiver, and vice versa. For instance, if one of them shares the key with an unauthorized party, the security of the entire cryptosystem will be ruined.

Modern day communicators say that these two concerns are extremely challenging. Nowadays, people are required to exchange valuable data with non-trusted and non-familiar parties (e.g. seller and buyer relationships). Because of these problems, cryptographers had to develop a new encryption scheme: the asymmetric key encryption.

Asymmetric Key Encryption

These cryptosystems use different keys for encrypting and decrypting the message. Although the keys involved are dissimilar, they still have a logical and/or mathematical relationship. It is impossible to extract the message using a decryption key that is totally unrelated to the encryption key.

According to cryptographers, this mode of encryption was developed during the 20th century. It was developed in order to overcome the challenges related to symmetric key cryptosystems. The main characteristics of this encryption scheme are:

- Each member of the cryptosystem should have two different keys – a public key and a private key. When one of these keys is used for encryption, the other one must be used for decryption.
- The private key is considered as confidential information. Each member must protect the private key at all times. The public key, on the other hand, can be shared with anyone. Thus, public keys can be placed in a public repository. As such, some people refer to this scheme as "public key encryption."
- Although the private and public keys are mathematically related, it is practically impossible to determine a key using its "partner."
- When Member1 wants to send information to Member2, he needs to do three things:
    - Obtain Member2's public key from the public repository.
    - Encrypt the message.
    - Transmit the message to Member2. Member2 will acquire the original message using his private key.
- This mode of encryption involves larger and longer keys. That means its encryption and decryption processes are slower compared to those of symmetric encryption.
- The asymmetric key encryption requires high processing power from the computers used in the cryptosystem.

Symmetric key encryption is easy to comprehend. The asymmetric one, however, is quite difficult to understand.

You may be wondering as to how the encryption and decryption keys become related and yet prevent intruders from acquiring a key using its "partner." The answer to this question lies in mathematical principles. Today, cryptographers can create encryption keys based on these principles. Actually, the concept of asymmetric key cryptography is new: system intruders are not yet familiar with how this encryption works.

Here is the main problem associated with asymmetric key cryptosystems:

- Each member needs to trust the cryptosystem. He/she has to believe that the public key used for the transmission is the correct one. That person must convince himself that the keys in the public repository are safe from system intruders.

  To secure the cryptosystem, companies often use a PKI (Public Key Infrastructure) that involves a reputable third party organization. This "outside organization" manages and proves the authenticity of the keys used in the system. The third party company has to protect the public keys and provide the correct ones to authorized cryptosystem members.

Because of the pros and cons of both encryption methods, business organizations combine them to create safer and practical security systems. Most of these businesses are in the communications and information technology industries.

Kerckhoff's Principle

During the 19th century, a Dutch cryptographer named Auguste Kerckhoff identified the requirements of a reliable cryptosystem. He stated that a cryptosystem must be secure even if everything related to it – except the keys – are available to the public. In addition, Mr. Kerckhoff established six principles in designing new cryptosystems. These principles are:

1. The cryptosystem needs to be unbreakable (i.e. in a practical sense). This excludes the system's vulnerability to mathematical intrusions.

2. The system should be secure enough that members can still use it even during an attack from unauthorized entities. The cryptosystem needs to allow authorized members to do what they need to do.

3. The keys used in the system must be easy to change, memorize, and communicate.

4. The resulting ciphertexts must be transmissible by unsecure channels such as telegraph.

5. The documents and devices used in the encryption system must be portable and easy to operate.
6. Lastly, the system must be user-friendly. It should not require high IQ or advanced memorization skills.

Modern cryptographers refer to the second rule as the Kerckhoff principle. They apply it in almost all encryption algorithms (e.g. AES, DES, etc.). Experts in this field consider these algorithms to be completely secure. In addition, these experts believe that the security of the transmitted message relies exclusively on the protection given to the private encryption keys used.

Maintaining the confidentiality of the encryption and decryption algorithms may prove to be a difficult problem. Actually, you can only keep these algorithms secret if you will share them with a few individuals.

Today, cryptography must meet the needs of internet users. Since more and more people gain access to hacking information and advanced computers, keeping an algorithm secret is extremely difficult. That means you should always use the principles given by Kerckhoff in designing your own cryptosystems.

Chapter 4: Different Types of Attacks on Cryptosystems

Nowadays, almost every aspect of human life is affected by information. Thus, it is necessary to safeguard important data from the intrusions of unauthorized parties. These intrusions (also called attacks) are usually classified based on the things done by the intruder. Currently, attacks are classified into two types: passive attacks and active attacks.

Passive Attacks

Passive attacks are designed to establish unauthorized access to certain pieces of information. For instance, activities such as data interception and tapping on a communication channel are considered as passive attacks.

These activities are inherently passive: they do not attempt to modify the message or destroy the channel of communication. They simply want to "steal" (i.e. see) the information being transmitted. Compared to stealing physical items, stealing data allows the legitimate owner (i.e. the receiver) to possess the information after the attack. It is important to note that passive data attacks are more harmful than stealing of physical items, since data theft may be unnoticed by the receiver.

Active Attacks

Active attacks are meant to alter or eliminate the information being sent. Here are some examples:

- Unauthorized modification of the message.
- Triggering unauthorized transmission of data.
- Modification of the data used for authentication purposes (e.g. timestamp, sender's information, etc.).
- Unauthorized removal of information.
- Preventing authorized people from accessing the information. This is known as "denial of service."

Modern cryptography arms people with the tools and methods for preventing the attacks explained above.

The Assumptions of a Cryptosystem Attacker

This section of the book will discuss two important things about system attacks: (1) cryptosystem environments and (2) the attacks used by unauthorized parties to infiltrate cryptosystems.

<u>The Cryptosystem Environment</u>

Before discussing the types of data attacks, it is important to understand the environment of cryptosystems. The intruder's knowledge and assumptions about this factor greatly influence his choices of possible attacks.

In the field of cryptography, three assumptions are made about the attacker and the cryptosystem itself. These assumptions are:

1. Information about the Encryption Method – Cryptosystem developers base their projects on two kinds of algorithms:

    i. Public Algorithms – These algorithms share information with the public.

    ii. Proprietary Algorithms – These algorithms keep the details of the cryptosystem within the organization. Only the users and designers can access information about the algorithm.

    When using a proprietary (or private) algorithm, cryptographers obtain security through obscurity. In general, these are developed by people within the organization and are not thoroughly checked for weaknesses. Thus, private algorithms may have loopholes that intruders can exploit.

    In addition, private algorithms limit the number of people that can join the system. You can't use them for modern communication. You should also remember Kerckoff's principle: "The encryption and decryption keys hold the security of the entire cryptosystem. The algorithms involved can be shared with the public."

    Thus, the first assumption is: "The attacker knows the encryption and decryption algorithms."

2. Obtainability of the Ciphertext – The ciphertext (i.e. the encrypted information) is transmitted through unsecured public channels. Because of this the second assumption is: "The attacker can access ciphertexts created by the cryptosystem."

3. Obtainability of the Ciphertext and the Plaintext – This assumption is more obscure than the previous one. In some situations, the attacker may obtain both the plaintext and the ciphertext. Here are some sample scenarios:

i. The attacker convinces the sender to encrypt certain pieces of information and gets the resulting ciphertext.

ii. The recipient may share the decrypted information with the attacker. The attacker obtains the corresponding ciphertext from the communication channel used.

iii. The attacker may create pairs of plaintexts and ciphertexts using the encryption key. Since the encryption key is in the public domain, potential attackers can access it easily. It's a "hit and miss" type of tactic.

Cryptographic Attacks

Obviously, every attacker wants to break into the cryptosystem and obtain the plaintext. To fulfill this objective, the attacker simply needs to identify the decryption key. Obtaining the algorithms is easy since the information is available publicly.

This means the attacker focuses on obtaining the secret decryption key. Once he/she gets this information, the cryptosystem is broken (or compromised).

Cryptographic attacks are divided into several categories. These are:

- BFA (Brute Force Attack) – Here, the intruder tries to find the decryption key by entering all possible information. For instance, the key contains 8 bits. That means the total number of possible keys is 256 (i.e. 2^8). The attacker tries all of these keys in order to obtain the plaintext. The longer the key, the longer the time needed for successful decryption.

- COA (Ciphertext Only Attack) – This tactic requires the complete set of ciphertexts used for a message. When COA gets the plaintext from the given ciphertexts, the tactic is considered successful. Attackers may also get the corresponding encryption key using this attack.

- CPA (Chosen Plaintext Attack) – This attack requires the attacker to work on the plaintext he/she selected for encryption. Simply put, the attacker has the plaintext-ciphertext combination. It means the task of decrypting the information is easy and simple. It is the first part of the attack – convincing the sender to encrypt certain pieces of information – that presents the most difficulties.

- KPA (Known Plaintext Attack) – With this tactic, the attacker should know some parts of the plaintext. He/she has to use this knowledge to obtain the rest of the message.
- Birthday Attack – This is a subtype of the brute force approach. Attackers use this tactic when working against cryptographic hash functions. Once the intruder finds two inputs that produce similar values, a collision is said to occur: the hash function is broken and the system is breached.
- MIM Attack (Man in the Middle Attack) – This attack is particularly designed for public key cryptosystems. In general, these systems require the exchange of keys before the actual transmission of the ciphertext. Here is an example:
    - Member1 wants to send a message to Member2. To do this, he sends a request for Member2's public key.
    - An intruder blocks the request and sends his own public key.
    - Thus, the unauthorized party acquires the information that will be sent by Member1.
    - To avoid detection, the intruder encrypts the data again and sends it to Member2.
    - The intruder uses his own public key. That means Member2 will see the attacker's key instead of Member1's.
- SCA (Side Channel Attack) – This attack is used to exploit the weaknesses of a cryptosystem's physical implementation. Here, the attackers ignore the system's algorithms and digital protection.
- Fault Analysis Attacks – When using this attack, the intruder looks for errors produced by the system. He/she uses the resulting information to breach the system's defenses.
- Timing Attacks – Here, attackers use the fact that different calculations require different processing times. These people can acquire some data about the message processed by a computer system. They do this by measuring the time used by the computer in performing its calculations.
- Power Analysis Attacks – These attacks are similar to the previous one. However, instead of time, they use the amount of power consumed by the

computer system. This information is used to determine the nature of the plaintext.

An Important Note About Cryptographic Attacks

The attacks explained above are theoretical and highly academic. Actually, most of those attacks are defined by cryptography instructors. Some of the attacks you read about involve unrealistic assumptions about the attacker and/or the system's environment.

However, these attacks have excellent potential. Attackers may find ways to improve them. It would be great if you will still consider these attacks when designing your own cryptosystems.

Chapter 5: Traditional Cryptography

You have learned about the basics of modern cryptography. You also discovered the different tools that you can use in designing your own cryptosystems. One of the powerful tools at your disposal is the symmetric key encryption: a mode of encryption that uses a single key for the entire communication process.

This chapter will discuss this mode further so you will know how to apply it in developing cryptosystems.

Old Cryptographic Systems

At this point, you have to study the cryptosystems used in the ancient times. These "old systems" share similar characteristics, which are:

- These cryptosystems are based on the symmetric mode of encryption.
- The message is protected using a single tool: confidentiality.
- These systems use alphabets to facilitate encryption. In contrast, modern cryptosystems use digital data and binary numbers to encrypt a message.

These old systems are called "ciphers." Basically, a cipher is just a group of procedures performed in order to encrypt and decrypt data. You may think of these procedures as the "algorithms" of these ancient cryptosystems.

1. The Caesar Cipher

This cipher is based on a single alphabet. Here, you can create a ciphertext just by replacing every letter of the message with a different one. Cryptologists consider this cipher as the simplest scheme today.

The Caesar Cipher is also called "shift cipher," since each letter is shifted by a fixed number. If you are using the English alphabet, you can use the numbers from 0 to 25. The people involved must choose a certain "shift number" before encoding the plaintext. The number will serve as the encryption and decryption key for the entire communication process.

How to Use the Shift Cipher

1. The sender and the receiver select a shift number.
2. The sender writes down the alphabet twice (i.e. a-z followed by a-z).
3. That person gets the plaintext and finds the appropriate letters. However, he moves the letters based on the shift number selected. For example, if

they are using the number 1, he will replace the letter "A"s with "B"s, the "B"s with "C"s, and so on.

4. The encryption procedure is done once all of the letters have been shifted.
5. The sender transmits the ciphertext to the receiver.
6. The receiver moves the letters of the ciphertext backwards, depending on the shift number being used.
7. Once all of the letters have been shifted, the decryption process is completed. The receiver can use the information he received from the sender.

The Cipher's Security Value

This is not a secure system since the possible encryption keys are extremely limited. If you are using the English alphabet, your possible keys are restricted to 25. This number is not enough for those who need more security. In this situation, an attacker may acquire your key just by carrying out a thorough key search.

2. The Simple Substitution Cipher

This is an improved version of the Caesar Cipher. Instead of using numbers to determine the ciphertext, you will choose your own equivalent for each letter of the alphabet. For instance, "A.C... X.Z" and "Z.X... C.A" are two simple permutations of the letters in the English alphabet.

Since this alphabet has 26 letters, the total permutations can be derived through this formula: $4x10^{26}$. The people involved can select any of these permutations to create the ciphertext. The permutation scheme serves as the key for this cryptosystem.

How to Use this Cipher

1. Write down the letters from A to Z.
2. The involved parties choose a permutation for each letter. For example, they might replace the "A"s with "F"s, the "B" with "W", etc. These new letters don't need to have any logical or mathematical relationship with the letter they represent.

3. The sender encrypts the plaintext using the selected permutations.
4. The message is sent to the receiver.
5. The receiver decodes the ciphertext using the chosen permutations.

The Cipher's Security Value

This cipher is way much stronger than the Caesar Cipher. Even strong computer systems cannot decode the ciphertext since the possible permutations (i.e. $4x10^{26}$) are too many. Cryptosystems based on this cipher can stop attackers that rely on a brute force approach. However, this substitution system is based on a simple scheme. In fact, attackers have succeeded in breaking letter permutations in the past.

The Monoalphabetic and Polyalphabetic Ciphers

Monoalphabetic Ciphers are ciphers that rely on a single encryption system. In other words, a single encryption alphabet is used for each "normal" alphabet throughout the entire communication process. For instance, if "C" is encoded as "X", "C" must be written as "X" each time it appears in the plaintext.

The two encryption systems discussed above belong to this type.

Polyalphabetic Ciphers, on the other hand, involve multiple encryption alphabets. The encryption alphabets may be switched at different segments of the encryption procedure. Here are two examples of polyalphabetic ciphers:

The Playfair Cipher

This encryption scheme uses pairs of letters to create encryption alphabets. Here, the people involved must create a table where letters are written down. The table used is a 5x5 square (i.e. 25 in total): the squares inside the table hold the letters of the alphabet. Since there are 26 letters in the English alphabet, a letter must be omitted. Cryptographers often omit the letter "J" when using this cipher.

The sender and the receiver must choose a certain keyword, say "lessons." They must write this keyword in the key table, from left to right. In addition, they should not repeat letters. Once the word is written down, the sender/receiver must complete the table using the unused letters (i.e. alphabetically arranged). With the word "lessons" as the keyword and J omitted, the key table should look like this:

L	E	S	O	N
A	B	C	D	F
G	H	I	K	M
P	Q	R	T	U
V	W	X	Y	Z

<u>How to Use this Cipher</u>

1. You should split the message into diagraphs (i.e. pairs of letters). If the total number of letters is an odd number, you should add a Z to the last letter. As an example, let's encrypt the word "human" using the key table created above. It will look like this:

   HU MA NZ

2. Here are the encryption rules:

   a. If both letters are in the same column, you should use the letter under each one. You have to go back to the top if you are using the bottom letter. In our example, N and Z are in the same column. Thus, this pair becomes FN.

   b. If both letters are placed in the same row, use the letter located at the right of each one. You need to go back to the first letter of the row if you are working on the rightmost letter. (This rule doesn't apply to our example.)

   c. If none of the previous rules apply, create a rectangle using the pair of letters. Afterward, use the letters on the opposite corner of the correct letters. Work on the letters horizontally. According to this rule, the HU pair is converted to MQ (look at the key table). MA, on the other hand, becomes GF.

3. Using these rules, the word "human" becomes MQ GF FN when encrypted using the Playfair Cipher.

4. You just have to reverse the process if you want to decrypt the message.

The Playfair Cipher's Security Value

This scheme is stronger than the systems discussed earlier. Attackers will have a difficult time analyzing all of the possible keys. In general, cryptologists use this cipher to protect important information. Lots of people rely on the Playfair Cipher since it is easy to use and doesn't require special tools.

The Vigenere Cipher

This encryption scheme uses a word (also known as text string) as the key. This key is used to change the plaintext. For instance, let's use the word "human" as the key. You should convert each letter into its numeric value (i.e. A = 1, B = 2, etc.). In our example:

H = 8, U = 21, M = 13, A = 1, N = 14

How to Use this Cipher

1. If you want to encrypt "cold water," you have to write the letters down. Then, write the key numbers (i.e. 8, 21, 13, 1, and 14) under the words, one number for each letter. Repeat the numbers as necessary. It looks like this:

C	O	L	D	W	A	T	E	R
8	21	`13	1	14	8	21	13	1

2. Shift the letters of the normal alphabet according to the number written on the table. Here it is:

C	O	L	D	W	A	T	E	R
8	21	13	1	14	8	21	13	1
K	J	Y	E	K	I	O	R	S

3. As you can see, each letter of the plaintext is moved by a different amount – the amount is specified by the key. The letters of your key should be less than or equal to that of your message.

4. To decrypt the message, you just have to use the same key and shift the letters backward.

The Vigenere Cipher's Security Value

This cipher offers excellent security: better than the three ciphers discussed above. Cryptographers use this encryption system to protect military and political data. Because of its apparent invulnerability, security experts call this the "unbreakable cipher."

Chapter 6: Modern Cryptography Schemes

Nowadays, cryptographers use digital data to establish encryption systems. This data is often represented as sets of binary digits (also called "bits"). Modern cryptosystems must process these binary strings to create more strings. Symmetric encryption techniques are categorized based on the procedures performed on the digital information. These categories are:

Block Ciphers

These ciphers group the digital data into separate blocks and process them one at a time. The number of bits contained in a data block is predetermined and unchangeable. Two popular block ciphers, AES and DES, have block sizes of 128 and 64, respectively.

In general, a block cipher uses a set of plaintext data and produces a set of ciphertext data, usually of the same size. Once the block size is assigned, it can no longer be modified. The block size used for the system doesn't affect the strength of encryption techniques involved. The strength of this cipher relies on the length of its key.

Block Size

Although you can use any block size, there are some things you have to consider when working on this aspect of your cryptosystem. These are:

- Avoid small block sizes – Let's assume that a block size is equal to m. Here, the total number of possible plaintext combinations is 2^m. If an intruder acquires the plaintext data used for previous messages, he/she can initiate a "dictionary attack" against your cryptosystem. Dictionary attacks are performed by creating a dictionary of ciphertext and plaintext pairs generated using an encryption key. You should remember this simple rule: the smaller the block size, the weaker the system is against dictionary attacks.

- Don't use extremely large block sizes – Large block sizes mean more processing time for your computer system. Cryptographers working on large bit sizes experience efficiency issues. Often, the plaintext must be padded in order to get the desired block size.

- Use a block size that is a multiple of 8 – Computers can easily handle binary digits that are multiples of 8. You can take advantage of this fact by choosing a block size that has this mathematical property.

Different Types of Block Cipher Schemes

Cryptographers use a variety of block cipher encryption schemes in their systems. Here are some of the most popular block ciphers being used today:

- AES (Advanced Encryption Standard) – This cipher is based on Rijndael, an award-winning encryption algorithm.
- IDEA – This is considered as one of the strongest ciphers available. Its block size is equal to 64 while its key size is equal to 128 bits. Many applications utilize this encryption. For instance, the old versions of PGP (Pretty Good Privacy) protocol used IDEA extensively. Because of patent issues, the utilization of this encryption scheme is restricted.
- DES (Digital Encryption Standard) – This is the most popular block cipher during the 1990s. Because of their small size, DES ciphers are now considered as "broken ciphers."

Stream Ciphers

With this scheme, the information is encrypted one binary digit at a time. The resulting ciphertext is equivalent to the data processed (e.g. 10 bits of plaintext produce 10 bits of ciphertext). Basically, stream ciphers are block ciphers with a block size limit of 1 bit.

Chapter 7: The Pros and Cons of Cryptography

This chapter will discuss the pros and cons of using cryptography.

The Pros

Today, security experts consider cryptography as one of their most useful tools. It provides four things needed for modern communication:

1. Authentication – Cryptographic techniques like digital signatures prevent spoofing and data forgeries.

2. Confidentiality – Encryption schemes protect information from unauthorized parties.

3. Non-repudiation – The digital signatures used in cryptography prove the identity of the sender. Thus, disputes regarding this factor are prevented.

4. Data Integrity – Cryptography involves hash functions that can maintain the integrity of the data being transmitted.

The Cons

Nothing is perfect. Here are the problems associated with cryptography:

- Legitimate users may encounter issues when accessing well-encrypted information. This can turn into a disaster if a certain piece of information has to be obtained quickly.

- Constant availability of information – a basic aspect of communications and information technology – is hard to secure when using cryptography.

- Cryptosystems prevent selective access control. Some organizations need to provide exclusive file access to certain officers. When using cryptosystems, these organizations will have problems in giving selective access to their chosen members. This is because cryptosystems apply the same security measures on every file.

Conclusion

Thank you again for purchasing this book!

I hope this book was able to help you master the basics of cryptography.

The next step is to build your personal cryptosystems so you can easily encrypt messages.

Finally, if you enjoyed this book, please take the time to share your thoughts and post a review on Amazon. It'd be greatly appreciated!

Thank you and good luck!

Book 3

Human-Computer Interaction

By Solis Tech

The Fundamentals Made Easy!

Table of Contents

Introduction

I want to thank you and congratulate you for purchasing the book, "Human-Computer Interaction: The Fundamentals Made Easy!"

This book contains proven steps and strategies on how to conceptualize and design a computer system that incorporate principles on effective interaction between the user and the device.

Human-computer interaction (HCI) is the study of the interaction between people and computers and the degree at which computers are developed enough to successfully interact with humans. So many institutions particularly academic and corporations now study HCI. Unfortunately, ease-of-use has not been a priority to most computer systems developer. The issue continues to bedevil the HCI community as accusations still abound that computer makers are still indifferent and are not making enough effort to make truly user-friendly products.

On the other hand, the designing task of computer system developers is not simple either as computers are very complex products. It is also true that the demand for use of computers have grown by leaps and bounds outstripping the need for ease-of-use by a significant margin. If you are a computer designer or simply have basic interest in making devices more effective for users, this book will help you a lot.

Thanks again for purchasing this book, I hope you enjoy it!

Chapter 1: Aspects of HCI

Main aspects of HCI

HCI is composed of three main features, namely: the user, the computer, and their interaction or how they work together.

"User" refers to either the individual or the group of users doing things together. An understanding of how the people's sense of sight, hearing, and touch send information is very important. Also, the type of mental models of interactions differs according to the personality of the user. And finally, interactions are also influenced by cultural and national differences.

"Computer," on the other hand, pertains to all technology from desktop to huge computer systems. As an example, if the topic is website design, the computer would then be the website. "Computers" would also include gadgets like mobile phones or even VCRs.

Finally, the "Interaction" is what happens as "User" uses the "Computer" to achieve a certain objective. Humans, of course, are totally different from machines. So the HCI's main intent is to ensure a successful interaction between the two.

In this aspect, adequate knowledge about humans and computers are critical to realize a functioning system. You need to seek inputs from users. Such knowledge would provide much needed information in determining schedule and budget that are crucial to the systems. In effect there are ideal situations and perfect systems. But the key is finding the balance between what is ideal and what is really feasible given the existing situation.

Objectives of HCI

HCI aims to come up with systems that are functional, usable, and safe. Developing computer systems with excellent usability depends on:

- having enough understanding of the aspects that lead people to use technology in certain ways
- being able to devise tools and ways for creating suitable systems
- the development of safe, effective, and efficient interaction

- making people the priority

The main philosophy underneath HCI is that the users or the people using the computers always come first. Developers must always be guided by the users' needs and preferences in designing systems. It is the system that should match the requirements of human users and not people changing to suit the nature of the machines.

The primacy of usability

Usability is one of the principal considerations in HCI. It is simply about ensuring that a system can be easily learned and used or be what is called user-friendly. A system is considered usable if it:

- can be learned easily
- can be remembered easily in terms of use
- is effective
- is efficient
- is safe
- is enjoyable

Lack of usability means wasted time, mistakes, and disappointments. Unfortunately, a lot of existing systems and devices have been designed without sufficient attention to usability. These include ATM, the Web, computer, printer, mobile phone, personal organizer, coffee machine, remote control, soft drink machine, ticket machine, photocopier, stereo, watch, video game, library information systems, and calculator.

A good example is the photocopier. If you are not familiar with the symbols on the buttons you will be greatly confused. For instance, the big button with the C on it actually refers to Clear, not Copy. The button used to produce copies is actually on the left side with an unrelated symbol. Devices and gadgets should be easy, effortless, and enjoyable to use.

Analyzing and designing a system based on HCI principles involve a lot of factors that produce really complex analysis because of interactions among many of them. The major factors are:

- The User – motivation, satisfaction, experience, enjoyment, personality. Also cognitive processes and capabilities

- User Interface – navigation, output devices, icons, commands, input devices, graphics, dialogue structures, user support, use of color, multimedia, natural language
- Environmental Factors – health and safety, noise, heating, lighting, ventilation
- Organization Factors – job design, work organization, training, roles, politics
- Task Factors – task allocation, skills, easy, novel, complex, monitoring
- Comfort Factors – seating, layout, equipment
- Constraints – budgets, buildings, cost, equipment, timescales, staff
- Productivity Factors – decrease costs, increase quality, increase innovation, increase output, decrease errors
- System Functionality – software, hardware, application

There are different disciplines representing a wide array of subjects that are covered in HCI. The manifold inputs from these fields have continued to enrich HCI. The disciplines include:

- Cognitive Psychology – limitations, performance predictions, information processing, cooperative working, capabilities
- Ergonomics – display readability, hardware design
- Computer Science – graphics, software design, prototyping tools, technology, User Interface Management Systems (UIMS) and User Interface Development Environments (UIDE)
- Social Psychology – social and organizational structures
- Engineering and Design – engineering principles, graphic designs
- Linguistics – natural language interfaces
- Philosophy, Sociology, and Anthropology – computer supported cooperative work (CSCW)
- Artificial Intelligence – intelligent software

Chapter 2: The Human Side in the HCI

Some of the key aspects that shed light on the human side of HCI are:

1. Perceptual-Motor Interaction. Effective human-computer interface design requires an appreciation of the whole human perceptual-motor system. The information-processing approach is central to the perceptual-motor behavior study and for considering the human factors in HCI. An effective interface design reflects the designer's knowledge of the perceptual such as visual displays, use of sound, and graphics. Also the cognitive exemplified by conceptual models and desktop metaphors as well as motoric constraints like ergonomic keyboards of the human perpetual-motor system.

   Man has gone beyond the use of computer punch cards and command-line interfaces. We now use speech recognition, eye-gaze control, and graphical user interfaces. The importance of various perceptual, cognitive, and motor constraints of the human system is now better recognized in HCI. An effective interface must take into account the perceptual and action expectations of users, the action that is seen with a response location, and the mapping of the perceptual-motor workspaces.

2. Human Information Processing. Aspects of human information processing such as models, theories, and methods are currently well developed. The available knowhow in this field is broadly useful to HCI in general such as in the representation and communication of knowledge and visual display design. An effective HCI requires making the interaction compatible with the human information-processing capabilities. Many things about human information processing have been integrated into cognitive architectures that are now applicable to HCI. These applications include the Model Human Processor, the Act model, the SOAR model, and the Epic model.

3. Mental Models in Human–Computer Interaction. Studying mental models can help understand HCI by inspecting the processes by which such models impact behavior. For example, mental models of machines can enable both novice and seasoned problem solvers to find new methods for fulfilling a task through more elaborate encoding of remembered methods.

   The Reverse Polish Notation is a great example of this. There is also a general theory that says readers develop a representation in their mind at several levels of what they read. First is the encoding of text, followed by the representation of propositional content of text. Finally, to this text, they integrate world knowledge to form a mental model of the situation described.

Readers also have the ability to look for ideas in multiple texts. They construct a kind of structured mental maps that show which documents contained which ideas even when they did not expect to need it while reading. Mental models are generally considered as semantic knowledge. Focusing on the degree of commonality among team members, for instance, when it comes to knowledge and beliefs, allows quantitative measures of similarity and differences which is the language of computers.

4. Emotion in Human–Computer Interaction. Emotion used to be persona non grata in the field of computer design. It had no place in the efficiency and rationality of computers which were the personification of zero emotion. Recent study findings in the field of psychology and technology show in a totally different light the relationship between humans, computers, and emotions.

   Emotion has ceased to be considered only in light of anger generated by inexplicable computer crashes or hyper excitement caused by video games. Nowadays, it is widely accepted that a host of emotions are important part of computer-related activities such as Web search, sending an email, online shopping, and playing computer games. In almost everything now, the emotional systems get engaged according to psychologists.

   Studies and discussions on emotion and computers have grown a lot because of dramatic advances in technology. Computers have actually been used to evaluate the relationship between emotion and its correlates. In the same vein, the astounding improvements in quality and speed of signal processing now enable computers to form conclusion on a user's emotional condition. Compared to purely textual interfaces that have very limited range, the multimodal interfaces that can use voices, faces, and bodies are now more capable to a broader range of emotions.

   Nowadays, the performance of an interface will be seriously impeded without considering the user's emotional state. Surprisingly, it can earn even descriptions like socially inept, incompetent, and cold. Much remains to be done to successfully incorporate emotion recognition into interfaces. Still, more studies about the interaction between design and testing can help create interfaces that are efficient and effective while providing satisfaction and enjoyment.

5. Cognitive Architecture. A cognitive architecture is a computer simulation program that makes use of human cognition principle based on human experimental data. It also refers to software artifacts developed by computer programmers. Likewise, the term also includes large software systems which are considered hard to develop and maintain.

Right now, cognitive architectures are not widely utilized by HCI practitioners. Nevertheless, it is quite relevant as an engineering field to usability and has important applications in computing systems especially in HCI. It also serves as theoretical science in human computer interaction studies. Finally, cognitive architectures combine artificial intelligence methods and knowledge with data and principles from cognitive psychology.

Presently-known cognitive architectures are undergoing improvements and are being utilized in HCI-related tasks. Two of the most well-known systems, EPIC and ACT, are production systems or built around one. All systems have production rules which differ from architecture to architecture. The difference lies on focus and history although there's a certain similarity in intellectual history. They may have more congruence than differences at some levels either because of mutual borrowings or due to the convergence of the science. The third system, Soar, is a bit different than the first two production system models.

The three production systems, Soar, Epic, and ACT-R were developed to present different types of human cognition but showed more similarities than divergence as they developed. It is not easy to describe a value possessed by architecture as advantage because to others it constitutes a disadvantage. For instance, Soar's learning mechanism is very important for modeling the improvement of users for a period of time. But there are many applications also where Soar's features result to harmful side effects that can cause more difficulty in model construction.

6. Task Loading and Stress in HCI. Stress in the form of task loading is central to HCI. The traditional perspective on stress sees it in light of exposure to some adverse environmental situations such as noise and the focus of attention centers on most affected physiological system. A new way of looking at it, however, stems from the findings that all stress effects are mediated through the brain.

   And since the brain is mainly focused on ongoing behavior or current task, stress ceases to be a peripheral issue but that the ongoing task becomes the primary source of stress. And this renders stress concerns that are central to all HCI issues. This means computer-based systems which aim at helping people lessen cognitive workload and task complexity actually impose more burdens and stress on them.

   The person's coping mechanism for such stress affects their work performance and personal wellbeing. The environment may vary but some mechanisms for appraising stress in all task demands are the same. So for HCI, certain principles and designs for stress are applicable across multiple domains.

There are several theories of stress and performance and their connection to human-computer interaction. Workload and stress are at times considered as varying perspectives on the same problem. There are some general practices for stress mitigation. But quite important for this topic is setting up effective measures of information processing and mental resources. It also includes expounding on task dimensions that are relevant and their relationship to self-regulatory mechanisms.

It is critical to establish how an individual's appraisal of his/her environment can be influenced by personal traits and states. This is because stress can only be understood vis-a-vis interaction between a person and the environment. Lastly, it is better to treat stress at multiple levels whether physiological or organizational when making practical application. Instead of one-dimensional which is bound to fail, multidimensional is better as it considers the person, task, and the physical, social and organizational environments.

The implication is that HCI researchers and practitioners should go beyond the design of interface displays and controls and focus also on the person aspects. What are the things in the individual that affect performance and the physical-social environment where the human-technology interaction happens? It means that the technical principles at work in that situation are not adequate. They cannot develop a complete description of the relationship between resources and cognitive activities.

7. Motivating, Influencing, and Persuading Users. From its former role as tool for scientists, the spread of computer use to all sectors of society has brought new uses for computers. Among those uses are persuading people to change their attitudes and behavior. Nowadays, it is widely accepted that skills in motivating and persuading people are necessary for developing a successful HCI.

   Interaction designers are actually agents of influence which unfortunately they have not yet understood and applied. Yet their works often involve creating something that tries to change people though they may not be conscious of it. Among these works are motivating people to register the software, learn an online application, or have product loyalty. Changing people's attitudes is now a common feature in the success of interactive products.

   Depending on the types of product, the persuasion factor can either be small or large. At any rate, anything that needs to be marketed needs to be persuasive. The growing use of computing products and the limitless scalability of software makes interaction designers one of the best potential change agents in the future.

Take for example the Web-interaction designers who increasingly are facing more challenge in designing something that will hold the attention and motivation of information seekers. After that, they need to persuade web users to adopt certain behaviors like:

- using a software
- joining a survey
- clicking on the ads
- returning often after bookmarking a site
- buying things online
- releasing personal information
- forming an online community

Being able to persuade people is a measure of success here. But with success comes responsibility. The Web designer needs to make the website credible. The following are some broad guidelines to ensure credibility:

1. Design websites to present the real and practical aspects of the organization.
2. Invest sufficiently in visual design
3. Make websites that people can easily use.
4. Include markers of good quality
5. Use markers of reliability.
6. Avoid too much commercialism on a website
7. Adopt and adjust to the user experience
8. Avoid being amateurish

To sum it all, computer systems have become an inescapable part of everyday life. The interactive experience involving all systems be it mobile phone or desktop can be designed in such a way as to influence the way we think and act. By combining the computing capability with persuasion psychology, computer systems can motivate and persuade. Humans are undoubtedly still superior when it comes to influencing people. But in many areas of endeavor, computer can do what humans cannot even imagine being capable of.

Computers don't sleep and can be designed to keep trying on and on. At the very least, computers provide a new way for modifying how people act and think. Like it or not, the community of HCI professionals is at the forefront of the campaign to make more sensitive and responsive tech products. It can rise to the challenge of helping churn out products that enhance the people's over-all quality of life. Or it can continue being a tool to produce mindless products whose main reason for being into is to make profit for the owners.

8. Human-Error Identification in Human–Computer Interaction. The leap from focusing on human error in technological problems to a less obvious culprit started in the 1940's. It was established during that year that plane pilot error was often designer error. It began to show that design is the key to

substantially reduce human error and this paradigm continued to gather steam particularly in HCI.

It is now common wisdom that human error can be as often as the product of a defective design or as a person making a mistake. The inadequate design fosters activities that lead to errors. A groundbreaking outcome of this new philosophy is that errors are now viewed as totally predictable events instead of seeing it as unpredictable occurrences. This makes errors avoidable.

So errors became instances where planned series of steps and activities fail to realize intended results independent of any outside change agencies. If errors are no longer random, then it can be identified and predicted ahead of time. What partially drove this line of thinking are the accidents that happened in the nuclear industry that is hungry for preemptive solutions. This has led to the formulation of several human-error identification (HEI) techniques.

Although evaluative and summative in nature, these HEI techniques that employ ergonomics methods can now be used in formative design stages especially in analytic prototyping. For instance, the entry of computer-aided design such as in architecture has profound impacts on prototyping. It made possible what was considered as impossible or too prohibitively costly design alteration at the structural prototyping stage.

The three main forms of prototyping human interfaces have been identified namely: functional analysis, scenario analysis, and structural analysis.

Functional analysis includes consideration of the functional range supported by the device. In comparison, scenario analysis is exemplified by consideration of the device in relation to events sequence. An example of the structural analysis, on the other hand, is the use of user-centered viewpoint in a non-destructive testing of the interface.

One compelling example of the crucial role of design in predicting and minimizing errors concern human error identification (HEI) tools like the TAFEI or Task Analysis for Error Identification. The results of the application of TAFEI on interface project designs show how it can improve systems and its relevance to other ergonomic methods. It served to validate what has been long suspected when it comes to error-design relationship as follow:

- Structured systems like TAFEI results to reliable and trustworthy error data;
- Most errors resulting from technology are totally predictable;

- To improve design and reduce errors, ergonomics methods should be employed in formative design process.

Exploring design weaknesses through tools like TAFEI will go a long way in developing and producing devices and gadgets that are tolerant to error.

Chapter 3: The Computer Side in the HCI

The salient points when it comes to the computer side in HCI include:

1. Input Technologies and Techniques. Input devices which are also a classification of computer can detect physical aspects of places, things, and, of course, people. However, its function is never complete without considering the visual feedback corresponding to the input. It is like using a writing instrument without something to write on. Input and output should always go together.

   And in devices with small screens, this is only possible with the help of integrated sensors. If the user or human characteristics are important in a maximized HCI environment, so are input technologies with enough sophistication to meet user-machine interaction requirements. Users can only achieve the task objectives by combining the right feedback with inputs. In this regard, the HCI designer should take into account the following:

a. the industrial and ergonomic design of the gadget

b. the physical censor

c. the relationship among all interaction techniques

Input gadgets have many properties that apply to the usual pointing devices or mobile items with touch input. These pointing devices include the: mice, trackballs, isometric joysticks, isotonic joysticks, indirect tablets, touchpads, touchscreens, and pen-operated devices. The mice or mouse, of course, is one of the most popular as anyone who has ever used a computer knows. Because of its inherent advantages for individual users where it can easily be used by most people, it is one of the most preferred pointing devices.

Touchpads are most well-known to laptop users. These are small tablets that are sensitive to touch and which are usually featured on laptop units. Touchscreens on the other hand are tablets that are sensitive to touch which are placed on a display. It is increasingly becoming the tool to beat because of the proliferation of smart phones and other hand-held devices.

There are input models and theories that are quite helpful in evaluating the efficacy of interaction strategies. But it would be most beneficial to readers here to focus on current and future trends for this feature. Interactive system designers should go beyond the usual things like graphical user interface and pointing ideas when it comes to inputs.

They must delve deeper into more effective search strategies, sensor inputs for new data types, and techniques of synthesis to make much better sense of data. Better search tools will enhance navigation and manual search regarding file systems. One outstanding development is the breakthrough in the development of more advanced sensor inputs such as technologies for tagging and location.

It allows computers to identify physical objects and locations that have been tagged, and to detect their location and distance to other devices through signal strength analysis. These sensors are making interface personalization much easier. This development in interaction also has great implications for data mining and techniques for machine learning. Continuous improvement in structure synthesis and extraction techniques is invaluable in this data-rich era.

An overriding aim in HCI is to achieve dramatic advancement in humanity's interaction with technology. The computer side of this presents limitless possibilities but the cognitive skills and senses of man will be relatively stagnant. Our holding, touching, and object-movement are not the result of technology-like progress but a product of our human limitations.

2. Recognition- and Sensor-Based Input for Interaction. Computers are able to manipulate physical signals that have been transformed by sensors into electrical signals. Sensors have found their way into various fields of industry such as robotics, automotive, and aerospace. It has also found vast applications in consumer products.

   The computer mouse is a very good example. Imagine that simple-looking device equipped with algorithms that process images and specialized camera that enables it to be unbelievably sensitive to motions. It detects movement at the rate of a thousand of an inch several thousand times per second. Another interesting device is the accelerometer that detects acceleration due to movement and continuous acceleration because of gravity.

   Digital cameras now make use of accelerometers to save a photo. Laptops also are equipped with accelerometers for self-protection. When the laptop is accidentally dropped the accelerometer enables the hard disk to secure the hard drive prior to impact. With smartphones, the goal is for motion sensing for the purpose of interaction such as determining the walking pattern of users. Generally, HCI research on sensors dwells on its usage to improve interaction.

   Sensor studies are either to broaden input options or build new computing forms. The new forms include mobile devices that recognize locations and places that are sensitive to the presence and needs of its inhabitants. Still there are far more advanced goals and applications like in robotics.

There is a race to develop machines that will behave and think like humans or at least complement their capabilities. It has many critical applications such as in nuclear power accident mitigation. One worry, of course, is that it will end up in the military. But in safety, mobile computing, entertainment, productivity, affective computing, and surveillance, sensors are finding widespread application.

An intriguing side note here is the idea of developing a sensor to enable computers to detect and accordingly react to the frustration of its user. The computer's response could be something like playing relaxing music. Sensing could be in the form of the user banging on the keyboard in frustration. A microphone could react to the yelling of the speaker or the webcam could sense scowling.

In general, the potential of interactive sensing is quite good. The degree of progress across the whole computing spectrum actually gives the impression that sky is the limit. Advances in nanotechnology, CPU power, and storage capacities will continue to produce more outstanding innovations in the computer side of HCI.

But what is driving the unprecedented growth of the sensor-based interactive systems is the dizzying expansion in devices outside the old desktop computer. It is hard to keep track of the explosive proliferation of smart phones, tablet PCs, portable gaming devices, music and movie players, living room-centric computers, and personal digital assistants. Computing is becoming part and parcel of our daily life and our environment.

Through recognition techniques and sensing systems, task-specific computing devices will be developed instead of general functions. It will also pave the way for different types of interaction style in HCI. This activity-specific interactive systems development will further hasten innovations on a much broader array of practical applications.

3. <u>Visual Displays</u>. Timekeeping has always been one function that man has strived for a good visual display. Today's smartwatches which are actually wrist computers sport stunning visual displays. It is no longer limited to displaying time but is multifunctional. Some brands can pinpoint exact location in the planet through a global positioning system. Others can show heart rate while a number can be personal digital assistants.

   The main idea behind wearable computing is that the human body is wearing the visual displays. One major way people use wearables is to put the display on one's head making user's hands free to work. It is called headmounted displays or HMDs. The screen-based is one category of HMDs. It makes use of the retinal-projection method which projects images on the retina of the eye.

An alternative method is the scanning displays which scan images onto the retina pixel by pixel. A second type of display which is actually much bigger in scope and the most widespread is the hand-held and wrist-worn displays. They are in mobile phones, media players, wristwatches, and other portable gadgets. Apple is one of the global leaders in this field and the most well-known. Even textiles for clothing are now being used for such technology in what is now known as photonic textiles-fabric.

Multicolored lighting systems were merged with the fabrics for its electronic information function without affecting the cloth's softness. It has sensors, GSM, and Bluetooth! Photonic fabrics have great promising applications in the areas of personal health care and communication.

4. Haptic Interfaces. Haptic interface refers to a device for sending feedback that produces sensation of weight, touch, rigidity, and other aspects through the skin and muscle. This force feedback mechanism is designed to enhance computer-human interaction. Because haptics are done through actual physical contact, they are not easy to synthesize unlike the sense of sight and sound that are gathered through the eyes and ears.

   The genius in the haptic interface is that it simply makes use of the body's own highly sophisticated receptor system. The haptic feedback is made possible through synthetic stimulation in the skin and proprioception.

   Proprioception involves something deeper than the skin – the muscle and skeleton. The mechanoreceptors in the body enable its detection of contact forces received from the environment. Body receptors sense velocity, skin stretching, vibration, and edges of objects. Haptic interfaces are more widely applied in the field of virtual reality than in information media and related devices are now available commercially.

Two of the most important research needs on haptic interfaces in the future concern the psychology in haptics and safety considerations. Safety is a crucial issue as insufficient actuator control can lead to injuries for users. Control problems may occur with the tool displays and exoskeleton. Unintended forces or vibration may pose danger to the user.

A locomotion interface that holds a user's body can cause serious physical damage if control is inadequate. It requires proven safety equipment that amply protects the walker and this should be a major objective of research. A much safer alternative is a system where the user does not wear any equipment during the interaction.

The psychology in haptics on the other hand requires more studies on muscle sensation as most existing findings are on skin sensation. Among the few promising findings relate to Laderman and Klatzky's work (1987) on force display and their recent study of forces distributed according to space. Their psychological findings have very promising applications in the development of haptic interface. A lot of obstacles need to be overcome before usage of haptic interface becomes widespread.

Though men cannot do without haptics in real life interaction, it is still of limited use in HCI. One can say haptic interface is still in infancy with its 10-year background. So eventually its time will come just like image displays (e.g. TV and movies) which started 100 years ago. For now, what are available are a few haptic interfaces with limited functionality and high cost. At the very least, haptic interface is a new very promising frontier in HCI with immense potential contribution to man's quality of life.

5. <u>Non-speech Auditory Output</u>. Sound is one of the key aspects that complete our interaction with our environment. But where speech is direct and necessitates focus and attention, non-speech sound is more diffused and provides a different class of information.

   Non-speech sounds include sounds from the environment, music, and sound effects. Nevertheless, speech and non-speech sounds complement each other just like text is complemented by visual symbols. Non-speech sounds can give information in a shorter period of time than speech.

   Right now, the non-speech field needs more research. The user interface is a much more effective tool for HCI when it employs a combined visual and sound feedback. This sound-visual combination has complementary function as well. Visual gives specific information about a small area reached by our eyes but sound or the auditory system provides more general information from beyond our focus.

   Our senses are the key to our effective interaction with the external world. These senses in turn bring more dimensions in information as they enhance one another. These principles are very useful in a multimodal HCI by adding non-speech sound output to the graphical displays. An example of this application is focusing our eyes on one task like editing a manuscript while monitoring other aspects in the machine through sound.

Reliance on visual sense which is more prevalent at present can be problematic. One problem is there could be visual overload which means the user could miss lots of information. Or simply that the viewer cannot look at everything at the same time at all times. Sound can help eliminate that situation by giving information to the user that the eyes could not see.

This interdependence between visual and audio could make information presentation far more efficient. Non-speech sound is mainly used in games' sound effects, music, and other multimedia usages. It is commonly employed in creating a certain mood for the item like in movies. In HCI, sound is used to provide information particularly those things that a user does not see or notice such as what is going on in their computer systems.

It is useful to use non-speech sound in HCI for many reasons. Seeing and hearing in the human body is first of all interdependent. The eyes can give information that is high-resolution only in a limited area of focus. But sounds can be received from all sides of the user: front, above, below, and behind. This not only provides direct information but also tells the eyes where to look to get more useful data. In fact, at times reaction to sound stimuli is faster than what is seen.

Non-speech sound can therefore help in reducing large display overload which can cause users to miss important data. This is especially true in large graphical interfaces that use multiple monitors. Using sound to present some information would reduce screen space. It would also lessen the volume of information that should be on the screen. This is most relevant to gadgets with small visual displays like smartphones and PDAs.

Non-speech sound would also decrease demands on our visual attention. For instance, a user who is walking would miss much information as he looks at his device's visual display because of competing attention from the traffic or uneven surface where he is walking. In fact, if the information is in sound, he does not have to look at his device at all.

Our sense of sound is also underutilized. Yet as exemplified by classical music, its intricate organization can make, say a symphony, a powerful tool for transmitting complex information. The beauty with sound is that it grabs attention. It is easy to avoid looking at something but hard to ignore sound which makes it very effective in sending important information. Likewise, certain things in the interface look more natural in sound than in sight.

Finally, non-speech sound will allow visually-impaired users to use computers. Newer graphical displays have, in particular, made it even harder for them to operate the device. Research has been extensive in the HCI application of non-speech sound in a wide range of topics.

There are two main areas of growth where the application of non-speech sound has the best potential. One is in the creation of multimodal displays that utilizes all available senses. This means integrating sound with other things like force-feedback and tactile apart from sight. The other area is in wearable and mobile computing gadgets that also use multimodal displays.

As mentioned, the screens of these devices are small and sound will reduce the need for screen space.

6. Network-Based Interaction. Networked interfaces have modified our perception of society and the world at large particularly with the Web and now mobile devices. There are several roles that networks play in HCI. The first is as an Enabler which refers to things that can be done only with network. The second is as Mediator which pertains to problems and issues caused by networks.

   Third is as Subject which focuses on managing and understanding networks and fourth as Platform which dwells on interface architectures and algorithms. Network includes both the wire-based and the wireless world. Things are rapidly changing especially in the wireless networks. These changes can be classified in two dimensions, namely:

- **Global vs. Local** – refers to the distance by space between the connected points such as machines in the office to global networks like the Internet.

- **Fixed vs. Flexible** – pertains to the nature of the links between points such as fixed devices and gadget that configures itself. More changes are coming because of spreading wireless links. One example is being able to gain access to internet connections and printers of another office by simply plugging a portable device into the Ethernet.

Traditionally, LANs belong to local-fixed category while Internet is global-fixed. Hand-helds like cell phones are also categorized as global-fixed because phones are fixed and independent of location. The internet makes use of domain names which are fixed like URLs. Some phone technologies like GSM and GPRS are classified as global-fixed because it is possible to send content that is based on location. Also the enlarging data capability is enabling services to handle huge media content.

What set these technologies apart, however, are the connectivity model and the charging which are usually by data use or fixed charge. There are a number of current and new technologies from the local-flexible type. These include the Wi-Fi, infrared, Bluetooth, and ZigBee which permit flexible connections among personal gadgets. With them, a computer device can utilize a mobile-phone modem or a headset with Bluetooth can make connections with a phone, wireless. Unfortunately, these capabilities also enhance unsavory activities like illegal equipment accessing, hacking, and surveillance.

7. Wearable Computers. Computers have become like appendage to many office workers. But it is hard for those using mobile devices to get the information

they need. In a mobile situation, existing interfaces will hamper the user's main task. Users will be forced to prioritize the device instead of the environment. The need is for a wearables design that helps fulfill not obstruct the task.

A framework that can be very useful in creating good designs of computer interfaces which are wearable is CAMP. This framework addresses different factors that may impinge on the effectiveness of the design such as body closeness and how it is used. CAMP stands for:

- Corporal – which means absence of discomfort to users during physical interface with the wearable.
- Attention – interface design should allow user to focus both on the real world and virtual reality.
- Manipulation – there are adequate controls which are easy to manipulate particularly in a mobile environment.
- Perception – Design must enable user to quickly perceive displays even when mobile. So displays should be easy to navigate and simple.

Outside offices and buildings, an attractive option for a user to have access to a computer interface is through wearables. There are challenges however that need to be addressed to fulfill the tasks in terms of contextual awareness, interface, adaptation to tasks, and cognitive model. These include:

- **Modalities of Input/output** – the ease of use and accuracy of modalities developed that try to copy the human brain's input/output capacity are not yet satisfactory. Frustrations bedevil users when there are inaccuracies. Also the computing requirement of these modalities is way beyond what low-weight wearable devices have. Input devices which are simple to use are needed.

- **Models of User interface** – there is a need for extensive experimentation in using applications involving end-users.

- **Capability-applications matching** – evaluation and design of interface should prioritize development of most effective way to access information and avoid creating additional features.

- **Simple methodology in interface evaluation** – current evaluation approaches are too complicated and time-consuming making them unsuitable in interface design. What is needed is an evaluation methodology that addresses frustration and human errors.

- **Context awareness** – for context aware computing to be realized, several questions must be answered. These include application models that integrate the social and cognitive aspects, social and cognitive mapping of inputs from many sensors, anticipating the needs of users, and interacting with the users.

Conclusion

Thank you again for purchasing this book!

I hope this book was able to help you to gain useful knowledge and understanding about human-computer interaction.

The next step is to apply what you have learned.

Finally, if you enjoyed this book, please take the time to share your thoughts and post a review on Amazon. It'd be greatly appreciated!

Thank you and good luck!

www.ingramcontent.com/pod-product-compliance
Lightning Source LLC
Chambersburg PA
CBHW061028050326
40689CB00012B/2735
9781530178094